Pacific Houses

Pacific Houses

Cynthia Reschke

HDi

HARPER
DESIGN
international

An Imprint of HarperCollins*Publishers*

Publisher: **Paco Asensio**

Editor: **Cynthia Reschke**

Editor in Chief: **Haike Falkenberg**

Texts: **by the architects**

Introduction and copyediting: **Ana G. Cañizares**

Documentation: **Cristina Montes**

Graphic design: **Agustín Argüelles**

Art Director: **Mireia Casanovas Soley**

Layout: **Gisela Legares Gili**

Copyright © 2004 by Harper Design International and LOFT Publications

First published in 2004 by:
Harper Design International, an imprint of HarperCollins Publishers
10 East 53rd Street
New York, NY 10022

Distributed throughout the world by:
HarperCollins International
10 East 53rd Street
New York, NY 10022
Tel.: (212) 207-7000
Fax: (212) 207-7654

HarperCollins books may be purchased for educational, business, or sales
promotional use. For information, please write:
Special Markets Department
HarperCollins Publishers Inc.
10 East 53rd Street
New York, NY 10022

Library of Congress Control Number: 2004101908

ISBN: 0060589108

DL: B-07482-04

Editorial project

LOFT Publications
Via Laietana, 32 4º Of. 92
08003 Barcelona. Spain
Tel.: +34 932 688 088
Fax: +34 932 687 073
e-mail: loft@loftpublications.com
www.loftpublications.com

Printed by:
Anman Gràfiques del Vallès, Barcelona, Spain

Summary

Introduction

No matter how many pictures of waterfront homes we may have seen leafing through the pages of books and magazines, they never fail to incite fascination, longing, and a great deal of envy. For those fortunate enough to own one, the images constitute a fruitful source of inspiration, as they do for architects and designers alike. This volume provides a refreshing new source of inspiration, focusing on houses situated along the world's largest body of water, the Pacific Ocean, whose unique and varying conditions produce efficient, dynamic, and impressive residential structures designed to harmonize with the natural landscape and cope with its often extreme conditions.

Named after its seemingly calm waters by the Portuguese explorer Ferdinand Magellan in 1520, the Pacific constitutes a total area of about 69 million square miles, covering one-third of the earth's surface. In other words, it is larger than the total land area of the world and is roughly 19 times the size of the United States. Located between the Western Hemisphere, Asia, and Australia, it is surrounded by a zone of violent volcanic and earthquake activity often referred to as the Pacific Ring of Fire. The monsoon season hits the western Pacific during the summer months, typhoons tend to strike southeast and east Asia from May to December, and hurricanes can form south of Mexico and Central America from June to October. The Pacific is home to the deepest known point in an ocean—the Mariana Trench, off the island of Guam, which plunges to a depth of about 36,000 feet, deeper than the highest point on Mount Everest. As a result of this depth, tsunamis are capable of reaching speeds of 470 miles per hour, the same velocity as a jet airplane.

The name that Magellan gave our biggest ocean can be deceiving, as it is not always as peaceful as it is beautiful. However, the Pacific's mystical quality, like that of any large body of water, has a powerful influence over our state of mind and reminds us of the sublimity of our existence. The peace it is capable of transmitting is the reason why anyone would give practically anything to own a house by the ocean. As a result, coastal architecture involves the careful design and selection of materials required to confront harsh climatic conditions, as well as the challenge of integrating a man-made element into Mother Nature, and the desire to make the most of the stunning views of the landscape. While some houses are situated on sand dunes, others are fastened to sloping hills or anchored to rocky terrain, making the task of architects that much more complex. The balance between material and concept, together with a genuine respect for the environment, produces spectacular residences that stand out for their design and their integration into such a powerful and contemplative setting as the Pacific coast.

Most of this planet we've never seen.
We are prisoners, confined to a measly one-third of its surface.

Graham Hawkes

How inappropriate to call this planet Earth when it is clearly Ocean.

Arthur C. Clarke

For whatever we lose(like a you or a me)
it's always ourselves we find in the sea

E. E. cummings

House in Ixtapa-Zihuatanejo

Situated at the edge of the Pacific Ocean, this house is located on the Grand Coast of Guerrero, Mexico. It is a rare setting in which the natural landscape and stunning views of the ocean are punctuated by surfacing rocks and small islands. A distinguished relationship between building and landscape generates an austere structure that defers to the overpowering vistas.

The balance between architecture and nature is evident in the overall design of the home. Composed of reinforced concrete and high-strength laminated glass, the house is defined by a large, central living area that incorporates the kitchen, dining area,

Architect: Enrique Muller
Interior Design: Mónica Hernández Sadurni
Photography: Angelo Destefani Hernandez (architect)
Location: Ixtapa-Zihuatanejo, Guerrero, Mexico
Date of construction: 2003
Area: 3,200 sq. ft.

and open-air terrace. Fully deployable glass doors open to join interior and exterior spaces, while skylights introduce additional light into the home. The predominant use of white, complemented by dark woods and accents of color by way of accessories maximizes the sensation of openness and luminosity.

The living areas and bedrooms enjoy panoramic views of the boundless ocean from various perspectives. The rounded pool spills over to create an infinite edge between pool and ocean, which are separated only by a stretch of transparent glass panels. The spacious outdoor terrace borders the water in a unifying gesture between architecture and landscape.

The balance between architecture and landscape is evident in the overall design of the home. Full-length glass panels offer transparent, uninterrupted views of the bordering water and distant horizon.

The bedroom is also oriented toward the ocean. A spacious living area incorporated into the bedroom acts as an extra lounge area or possible guest bed.

Yorkin House

This project evolved in response to two main characteristics of the surrounding site. On one side, the Pacific Coast Highway carries streams of commuters and leisure traffic with the attendant noise and bustle. On the other, the sandy Pacific beaches provide a stunning and infinitely transforming panorama.

The house presents a bold sculptural presence to the highway, where it receives only indirect light. The rooftop is animated by light scoops and provides a habitable landscape for spectacular views and protection from breezes. A series of layers leads to the entrance courtyard of native beach grasses over a wooden boardwalk. Inside, the house is layered from more internally focused

Architect: Moore Ruble Yudell Architects & Planners
Collaborator: Marc Schoeplein, Project Architect
Photography: Kim Zwarts and Tim Hursley
Location: Malibu, California, USA
Date of construction: 1999
Area: 7,500 sq. ft.

family areas to open light-filled social spaces that communicate through sliding glass walls to an exterior courtyard, terrace and the beach beyond. Stairs weave vertically through this layering to bring color, light, and openness from above.

The house functions as a retreat for the owner, her two adult children, and their families. In spite of the urban density of the site, the courtyard typology and flexible walls allow for multiple configurations. The dynamics of the space allow for equal comfort in accommodating one person or many, and can be used for a full spectrum of activities from formal to informal throughout all seasons. The house's relationship to the site is expressed by the urban character of the highway, the open marine character of the terraces and decks, and the carefully framed light and views. This connection to place is enhanced by colors of sand and beach and by the native plants of the gardens.

The configuration of this structure is defined by the contrasting landscapes that flank the property: the urban character of the highway on one side, and the marine character of the open terraces and decks facing the ocean on the other.

19

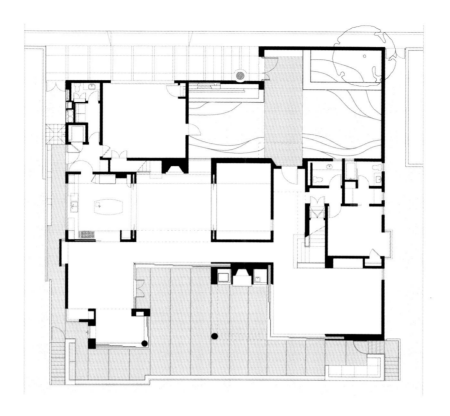

Ground floor

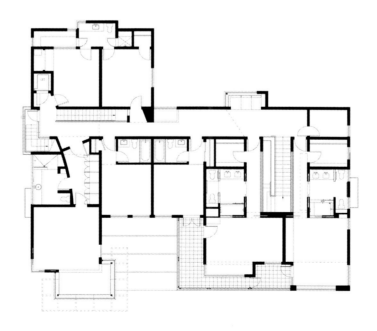

First floor

0   2   4

Malibu Residence

The program for this project involved the renovation of an original 1967 dwelling into a structurally reinforced, contemporary urban retreat. Perched along Malibu's Pacific Coast Highway, this modern house enjoys direct access to the beach from behind. A transitional interior entry courtyard, laid with rectangular cement pavers and bordered by smooth river rock and tufted grasses, introduces the primary design element of the home—a seamless union between interior and exterior spaces, linear architecture, ambulating plan, and visual access throughout.

From the courtyard, an original space accented by a white grid of window panes contains the dining room. The graphic grid is echoed by the geometric pattern created by the cabinets and shelves that lead into the minimal kitchen. True to the open plan,

Architect: Shubin + Donaldson Architects Inc
Photography: Tom Bonner
Location: Malibu, California, USA
Date of construction: 2001
Area: 3,400 sq. ft.

the kitchen seamlessly overlooks the main living space. The interior design palette of natural woods and limestone, white walls and fabrics, and frosted and clear plate glass generates a crisp and airy environment that allows the appreciation of the Pacific Ocean setting. Openness and transformation are themes throughout, and are most expressive in the master bath. Ocean blue frosted glass and additional glass layers heighten this sensation of space and transparency. Dark wenge wood was used to accent certain pieces in order to contrast them with the limestone counters and floors.

The ground floor living room and adjacent sitting room offer a serene respite from the sunlit terraces beyond, with cooling light and the dark wood tones of the furniture and materials employed. Double-paned windows, which open onto the first-level terrace, offer uninterrupted views of the exterior, while also acting as a buffer from the traffic noise.

Glass comprised the main ingredient of the design of this Malibu home. Its privileged location, right on the beach, was optimized to obtain the best views of the shore and introduce as much light as possible into the home.

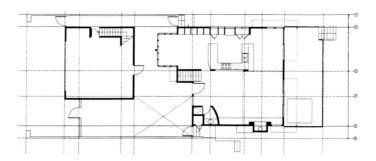

Ground floor

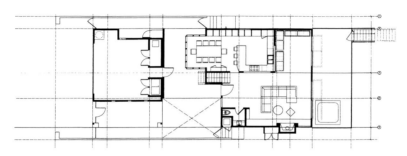

First floor

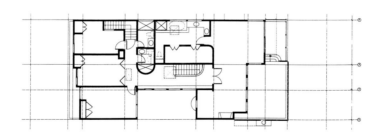

Second floor

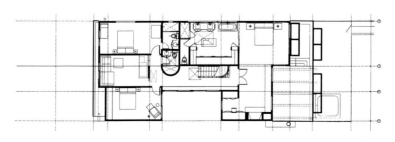

Third floor

0   2   4

Sliding full-length glass doors are one of the most common features in waterfront homes, enabling a seamless and practical connection to outdoor patios or terraces.

Eastern View Beach House

Hayball Leonard Stent was engaged to design a beachside residence along the Great Ocean Road, Victoria. As one of the premier tourist destinations along the Victorian coastline in southeast Australia, the area overlooks the unruly Bass Strait, which separates the mainland from the island state of Tasmania. The site is exposed to extremely cold storms blown in from Antarctica during the winter, while summer can be characterized by long hot days on the beach and cool winds in the afternoon, tainted only by the ever present threat of bushfire. The most recent occurred in 1985, when the Ash Wednesday fires ravaged the area and the adjoining state forest.

The client for the project is a fashion designer who has an adolescent daughter and runs a successful business. Her goal was to provide separation from the hectic business part of her life and offer balance, capitalizing on the powerful natural environment and forces in which the site indulges. In contrast with much of the housing built in prominent locations, this house does not

Architect: Hayball Leonard Stent Architects Pty Ltd
Photography: Peter Clarke
Location: Eastern View, Victoria, Australia
Date of construction: 1999
Area: 3,330 sq. ft.

perform structural gymnastics to maximize views in a resultingly obtrusive form. Rather, the structure falls behind the primary dune and follows the natural gradient of the sloping terrain. Shielded at the back by a state forest, the house is invisible from passing traffic, creating privacy and seclusion.

The design responds to the opportunities of the site, maximizing the views provided by the topography. The sequencing of spaces primarily organizes the house into two separate wings. Living spaces open out toward the ocean, while the bedrooms enjoy the protected northern view of the forest. External materials were treated to withstand the rigorous coastal climate. Both the interior and the exterior of the building adopt a contemporary architectural image, conforming appropriately to the strict council design guidelines over siting, material, and color.

Straightforward architecture and simple lines generate an elegant and modern home that defers to the surrounding views of the landscape. The bedrooms were oriented toward the more protected view of the forest, while the living area looks out toward the water.

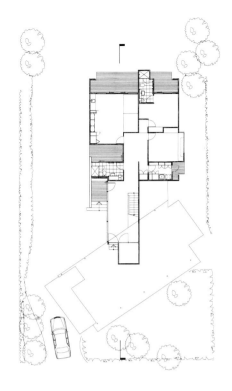

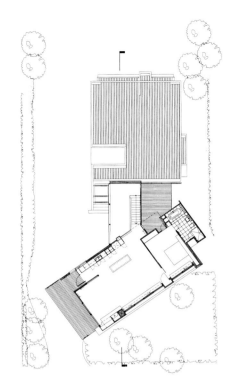

Ground floor

First floor

0 2 4

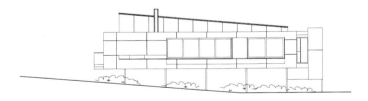

Section

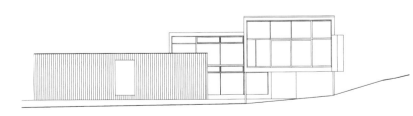

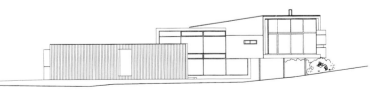

Elevations

0 3 6

Montecito Residence and Guesthouse

The residence and guesthouse are situated in the gently sloping foothills of Montecito, California, enjoying panoramic views of the Santa Barbara Harbor, the Pacific Ocean, and the surrounding mountains. The irregularly shaped site affords many views and privacy to the interior spaces. Introducing the structures into the land and disturbing the natural landscape as little as possible were the most critical aspects of the design plan.

A serpentine driveway and garden wall lead from the street entry gate to the motor court at the front of the main house, which is a two-story contemporary villa with extensive terraces and lawns for relaxed indoor and outdoor living. The design consistently addresses the owners' desire to achieve a simple and elegant environment with abundant daylight and dynamic views. A 50-

Architect: Ronald Frink Architects Inc
Photography: Benny Chan/Fotoworks and Erhard Pfeiffer
Location: Montecito, California, USA
Date of construction: 2001
Area: 3,952 sq. ft.

foot bridge links the infinity pool and spa terrace of the main house, through a canopy of oak trees, to the 800-square-foot guesthouse, in the secluded the privacy of an acacia grove. This two-story volume features full-height windows and a curved bay window that provide wonderful light and filtered views through the trees of the ocean horizon.

A 1950s jukebox and soda fountain are incorporated into the custom millwork of quartered maple along with the entertainment center and bar area. The railings and cabinet hardware are brushed stainless steel, and recessed lighting allows the guesthouse to glow like a lantern in the evening. A spiral staircase leads to the sleeping loft and powder room above. The new addition offers an informal, private retreat from the main house, which, in spite of its small size, is both uplifting and expansive.

This irregularly shaped site affords varying perspectives of the harbor, ocean, and surrounding mountains. A landscaped garden and pool integrate the linear structure into the natural environment.

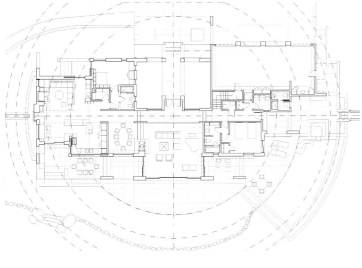

Main house ground floor

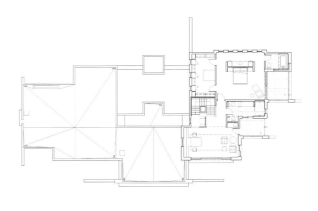

Main house first floor

0   2   4

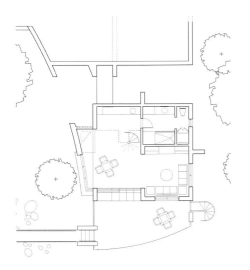

Guest house ground floor

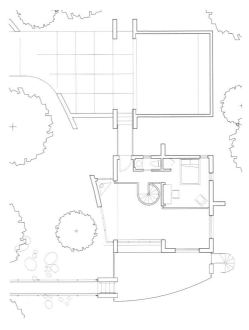

Guest house first floor

51

Port Fairy House

Located in Port Fairy, Victoria, this house is nestled in the sand dunes and tea tree scrub just 165 feet from the shoreline of the beach. With its numerous outdoor living options, the house is designed to protect the occupants from the winds while allowing in abundant sunlight.

The form of the house is inspired by purity and simplicity, on a relatively large scale. The majority of Farnan Findlay architects are passionate about the idea of a beach house or retreat, but believe that it should never resemble a townhouse by the sea, whose

Architect: Farnan Findlay Architects
Photography: Brett Boardman
Location: Port Fairy, Victoria, Australia
Date of construction: 2003
Area: 3,200 sq. ft.

typical extensive lawns and patriotic symbolism can be seen destroying the charm and natural settings of many towns along the New South Wales coast. The Port Fairy house could never be construed as urban. The building, clad in painted eucalyptus shiplap boards and supported by a rendered brick base, employs unconventional spaces that are in constant transition.

Outdoor spaces are contained in the form of the building. The upper decks are completely exterior, yet designed as interior rooms. Many different outside spaces are opportunities for outside living, designed to suit the weather conditions or the position of the sun. The corner windows capture the setting and glimpses of distant features such as the lighthouse and the battered western coastline. A rooftop observation deck affords 360-degree views of the picturesque township with its huge Norfolk Island pines and bluestone buildings, as well as an opportunity to check out the surfing or diving conditions before heading out to the beach.

The upper outdoor decks were designed as interior spaces, and appear as if the ceilings had been simply cut out. Extendable screens were incorporated to provide shade when necessary.

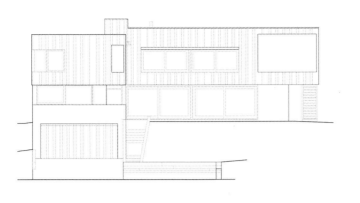

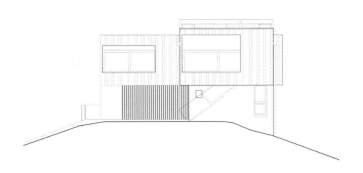

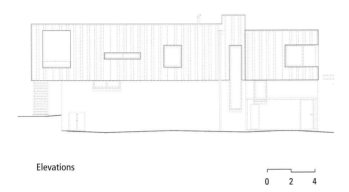

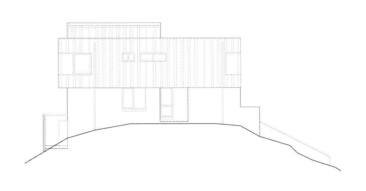

Elevations

0   2   4

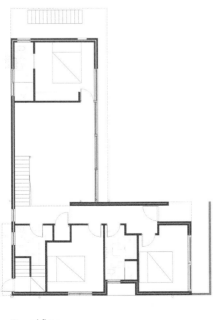

Ground floor

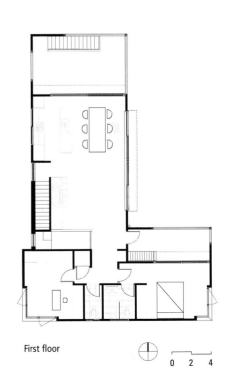

First floor

0   2   4

Clement Residence

In approaching the design of this single-family dwelling in Venice, California, the architects chose to explore the relationship between the interior spaces of a living environment and the exterior contextual condition. Conceptually, the windows become a means of capturing the outdoor landscapes and introducing them onto the building surface to enhance the interior experience. Because the lot is snugly set into its context, the adjacent structures were critical in developing the interior spaces. In order to create the most advantageous views, the architects considered the ancient Japanese garden design practice of using a borrowed landscape. In traditional Zen gardens, designers would often create barriers that would obscure an unwanted foreground to emphasize an immediate connection of the microcosm of the garden with a mountain or any other natural landscape in the background. This editing of the user's view reinforced the abstract reading of the garden, in which each element stands in for a larger whole in nature.

Architect: Eric Rosen Architects Inc
Photography: Erich Ansel Koyama
Location: Venice, California, USA
Date of construction: 2001
Area: 3,600 sq. ft.

In this project, the architects have inverted this technique, in light of the absence of any sublime scenery on the horizon. The location, shape, and orientation of each of the rooms were thoughtfully designed to frame specific views, and thus constitute a carefully edited piece of nature as it relates to the different site adjacencies. Placing the bedrooms at the front in order to mask the street allows the common living spaces to flow into the more private and secluded backyard. Whether it is a slice of sky, a boulder placed just outside in the back garden, or a flower bed, each opening presents a carefully framed piece of nature or exterior condition. The result is a multifaceted house that acts as a visual screen, selecting bits of nature that the user can admire to experience a closer relationship with the surrounding atmosphere.

In this house, surrounded closely by neighboring buildings, the shape and orientation of each of the rooms were carefully designed to frame specific views so that the resident could experience a closer relationship with the exterior landscape.

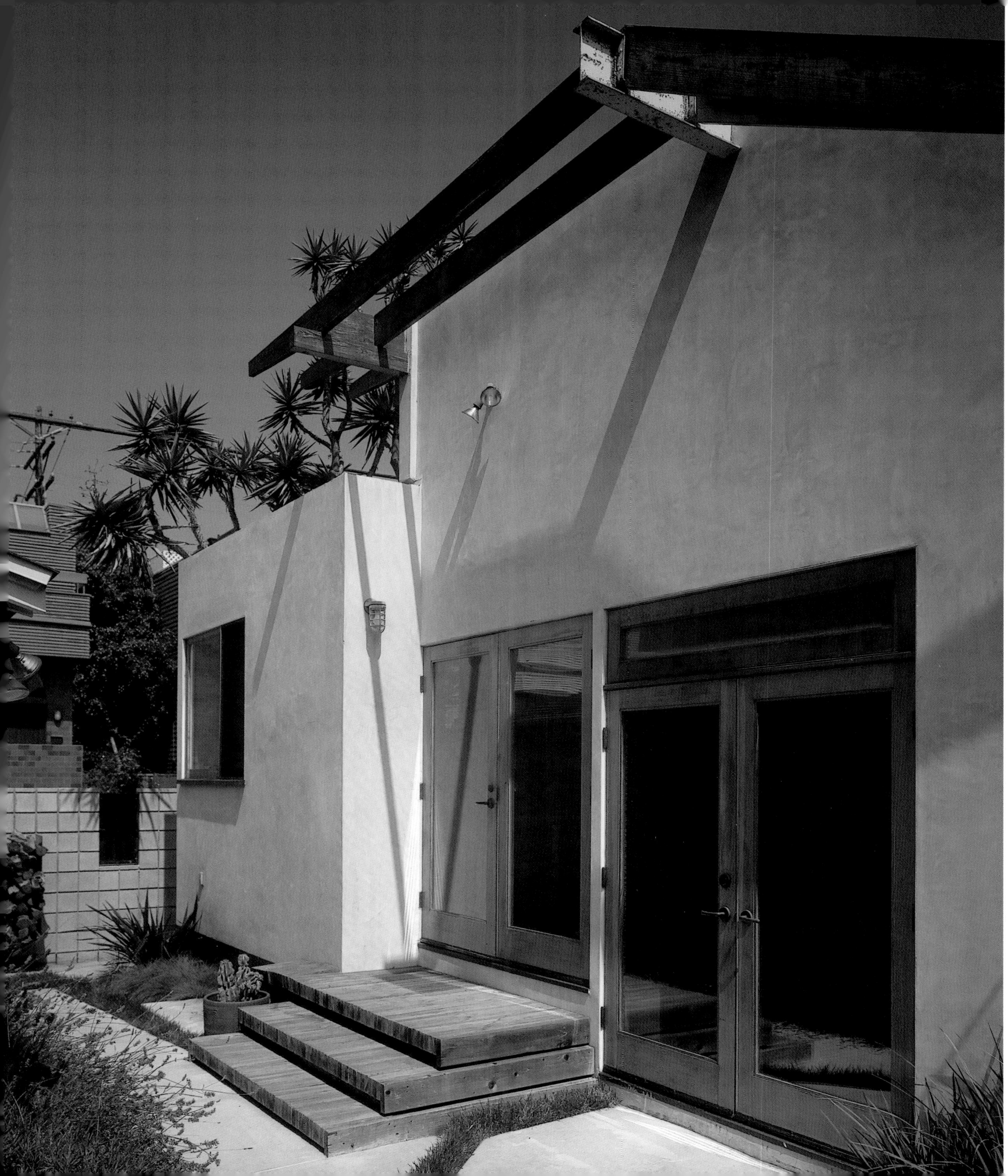

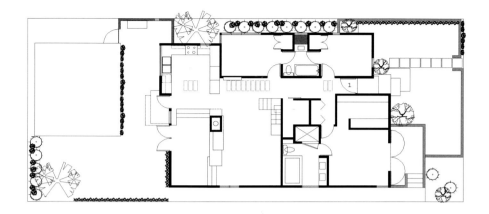

Ground floor

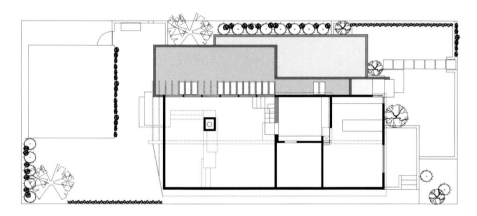

Loft

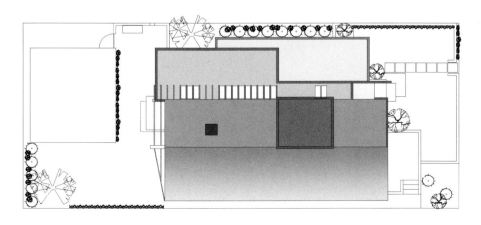

Roof

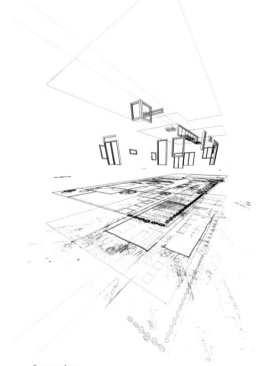

Perspectives

The public zones inside the home adopt an open-plan distribution and are defined by an integrated fireplace and entertainment unit that separates the living room from the dining area.

Residence for a Photographer

This apartment for a photographer is an addition to an existing industrial structure located on San Francisco's Potrero Hill. The owner had previously converted the former paint factory into his commercial photography studio and now wanted a small residence connected to the building, but removed from his working space. The addition to the original single volume, built in concrete with bowstring wood trusses, sits above the existing photography studio, with views of the city skyline and San Francisco Bay.

The apartment is organized as a sequence of spaces at different levels: the ground floor studio, an intermediate mezzanine, the roof-level living spaces, and a rooftop exterior deck. These spaces become increasingly light, open, and extroverted as one ascends

Architect: Leddy Maytum Stacy Architects
Photography: Stan Musilek, Sharon Reisdorph
Location: San Francisco, California, USA
Date of construction: 1997
Area: 1,175 sq. ft.

from the dark, enclosed photography studio. A metal stair leads to the new mezzanine level, in which bowstring trusses are positioned just under the existing curved roof and above the studio below. In the living space, large sliding glass panels frame the city view to the north. When these are opened, the living area extends out to include a narrow exterior deck.

The new elements are lightweight construction designed to relate to and also contrast with the masonry and heavy timber structure of the original building. The galvanized metal exterior of the addition is an extension of the existing silver-coated roof. In contrast to the monochromatic metal exterior, interior finishing materials include colored concrete countertops, glass tile, sandblasted glass, stainless steel, maple cabinetry, and maple flooring. On the whole, the photographer can experience the residence as an exploration of construction, light, openness, and spectacular views.

A sundial adorns this impressive entrance that leads into the photographer's home, characterized by materials like stainless steel, wood, and glass.

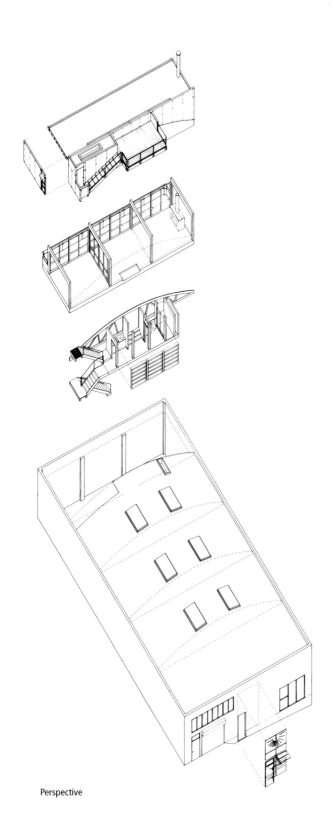

Perspective

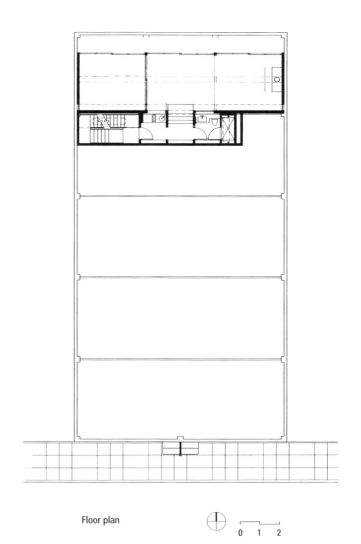

Floor plan

0 1 2

The kitchen and bathroom are compact, leaving abundant space for the living area and bedroom, which are divided by a sliding translucent screen framed in stainless steel.

Yudell-Beebe House

This house was developed in close response to the rhythms and materials of the rugged coast of northern California. Close to a coastal bluff, the site falls under strict architectural guidelines. The architects sought to embrace the fundamental environmental intentions of the guidelines while creating a contemporary place of strong individual character and quiet complexity.

Each part of the house responds to specific conditions of the site. The east elevation presents a rugged entry—a contemporary interpretation of the western front. The west provides screening from houses across the meadow while framing water and rocks

Architect: Moore Ruble Yudell Architects & Planners
Photography: Kim Zwarts
Location: The Sea Ranch, California, USA
Date of construction: 2000
Area: 2,460 sq. ft.

through habitable bays. The south opens to the ocean with full or partial shading, and the north is shaped as an intimate court with mountain views. A garden of native grasses and rocks suggests the link between mountain and ocean, with an implied passage though the heart of the home.

Movement through and around the house is choreographed to enhance the spatial and sensorial experience. Windows are composed to frame near and distant landscapes and to celebrate the movement and wash of light. The courtyard, which faces northeast, catches the morning sun and at the same time screens the prevailing winds; the towers of the studios, reaching their 16-foot height limit, also collect incoming light rays. Configured so that all spaces have multiple exposures to the exterior, the rooms optimize daylight and ventilation. Spaces in simple shapes shift dramatically in height and present a layered sequence of framed views and paths. These characteristics maintain a continual and dynamic dialogue with the everchanging landscape, celebrating craft and place as a retreat for quiet contemplation or spirited social interaction.

This linear structure is configured so that the interior spaces experience multiple exposure to the exterior and receive plentiful daylight and ventilation. The simple, boxlike shapes shift dramatically in height and are layered to create a sequence of framed views and paths.

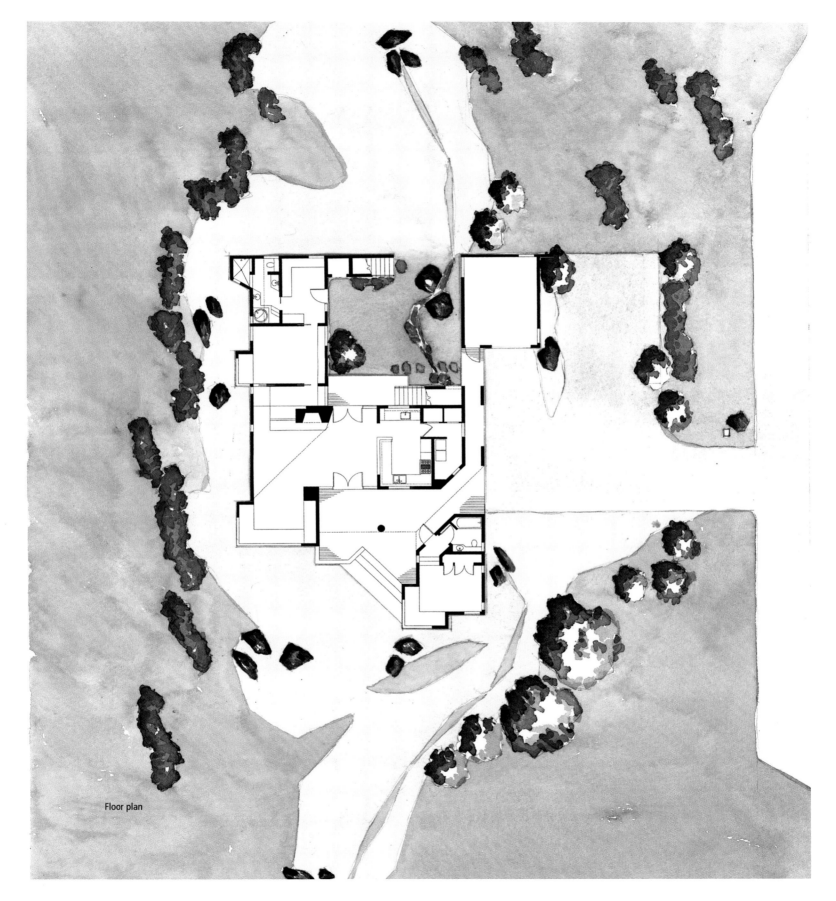

Floor plan

Stone Hill Residence

Located in the Santa Monica Mountains, the Stone Hill residence was conceived as two separate structures connected by an interior bridge. The two buildings are massed separately and recognized by folding layers of metal roofing. At the volumetric intersection, seamless glass clerestory windows allow for the uninterrupted identification of each mass and the entry of light into the center of the living space.

The residence is 3,000 square feet with an open plan upper level, allowing unimpeded transition of space between the living room, dining room, family room, and kitchen. The lower level hovers three feet above the exterior patio and pool, and consists of three

Architect: Belzberg Architects
Photography: Hagy Belzberg
Location: Brentwood, California, USA
Date of construction: 2000
Area: 3,000 sq. ft.

bedrooms that communicate with the upper level via a floating staircase. Wood furnishings predominate, as does the extensive use of glass to afford light and amplify the views obtained from the house's elevated position. Deployable glass doors transform the living room into an open-air terrace, and sliding partitions offer the possibility of rearranging the public zone in various ways.

The main decorative element is the structure itself—a steel frame construction—exposed to reveal the scale of each building and its intersecting condition. Steel trowel plaster, metal roofing, and aluminum window frames complete the exterior envelope. The upper level interior space is distinguished further from the exterior by "wood clouds," framed down from the ceiling to identify internal spaces such as the kitchen, dining, and lounge areas.

The sloping roof planes and unusual configuration of this structure are the distinctive features that make it unique.
The steel frame construction is exposed to reveal the scale of each building and its intersecting condition.

Casuarina Beach House

The concept of this home is that of an open, breezy, relaxed, and extroverted living pavilion, juxtaposed with a two-story shuttered timber sleeping box. The aim of the architects was to integrate the house into the whole site by pushing parts of the building fabric out to the extremities of the site and capturing external space within various levels of enclosure. The house also incorporates a strong environmental program that serves as a prototype for sustainable living in beachside communities.

The most challenging aspect of the brief was to answer to the site, having been built on a rejuvenated greenfield site and providing little context to respond to. Extensively sand mined in the 1970s and replanted with mostly fastgrowing and noxious

Architect: Lahz Nimmo Architects
Collaborators: Peter Titmuss, Tim Horton, Marcus Trimble
Photography: Lahz Nimmo Architects
Location: Casuarina Beach, New South Wales, Australia
Date of construction: 2002
Area: 3,600 sq. ft.

exotics, this house was one of the first buildings to be completed. While the house currently sits within a large open site, it was designed with future subdivision in mind, responding to a relatively narrow allotment.

The main two-story bulk is pushed away from the beach and dunes toward the street to preserve oblique views of the beach from future neighbors. The street side of the house acts as the formal public interface, and deals with the functional aspects like driving in and parking vehicles. Situated in a climatically dynamic and changeable environment, the house, like a boat, must be able to open and close in relation to the fluctuating weather patterns. In this way, the sleeping box has a series of shutters and timber louvers that open and close depending on the daylight requirements. A double height breezeway space leads into the living pavilion, serving as an entry and sheltered deck area. The materials used were generally detailed and finished to express and celebrate their inherent nature.

The design of this sustainable home is based on the concept of an open living pavilion as the main public area, juxtaposed with a two-story sleeping box as the private area in which the bedrooms are located.

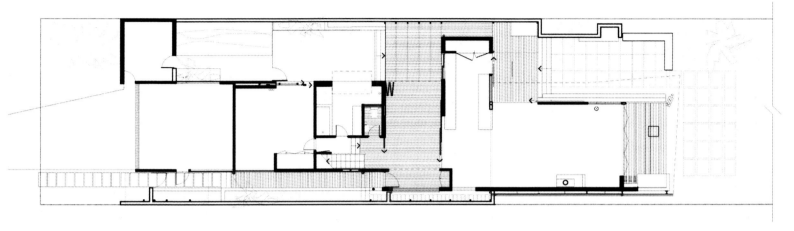

Ground floor

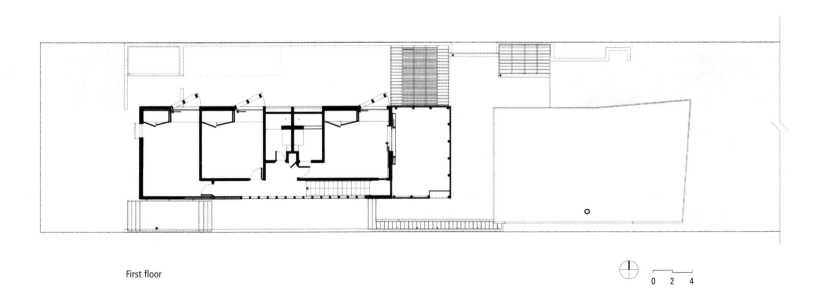

First floor

0 2 4

House in Wakayama

The design of this house in Wakayama revolves around the concept of the traditional Japanese *tsuboniwa*, or "small garden."
Tsuboniwa is a Japanese tradition of small gardens that can be made in spaces of one *tsubo*, the equivalent of 36 square feet.
Said to have originated in ancient Kyoto within temples, households, and other structures, this concept involves a studied balance
of elements between water, plants, rocks, and art objects. Many city dwellers in Japan continue to employ and re-create this
concept as a way of remaining connected to the natural world amid an urban setting.

In this case, the architects aimed to challenge the traditional notions of this garden by transforming it into a "forbidden" one.
Whereas tradition holds that nature is introduced into the building and domesticated into a microcosm, in this project, nature is

Architect: Waro Kishi + K. ASSOCIATES/Architects
Collaborators: Urban Design Institute, Umeda Mechanical Design Office
Photography: Hiroyuki Hirai
Location: Wakayama, Japan
Date of construction: 2002
Area: 3, 658 sq. ft.

abstracted, consisting of only one tree as the vertical element and a water plane as the horizontal element. By converting it into
a water garden, the resident is prohibited from entering the courtyard, and therefore prohibited from coming into contact with
nature itself. It is a forbidden garden that encloses a natural space almost as if it were to be admired and venerated, rather than
walked through.

Flanked by glass on both the lower and the upper levels of the house, the garden is the focal point of the project and visible from
practically anywhere in the home. A footpath punctuates the garden from one side to the other, seemingly floating along the still
surface of the water. Steel, glass, and white tones define the austere and Zen-like environment of the house.

Conceived around the abstraction of the traditional concept of the Japanese garden, the design for this home brings
together two very characteristic elements of the Japanese culture: mixture of modern and tradition.

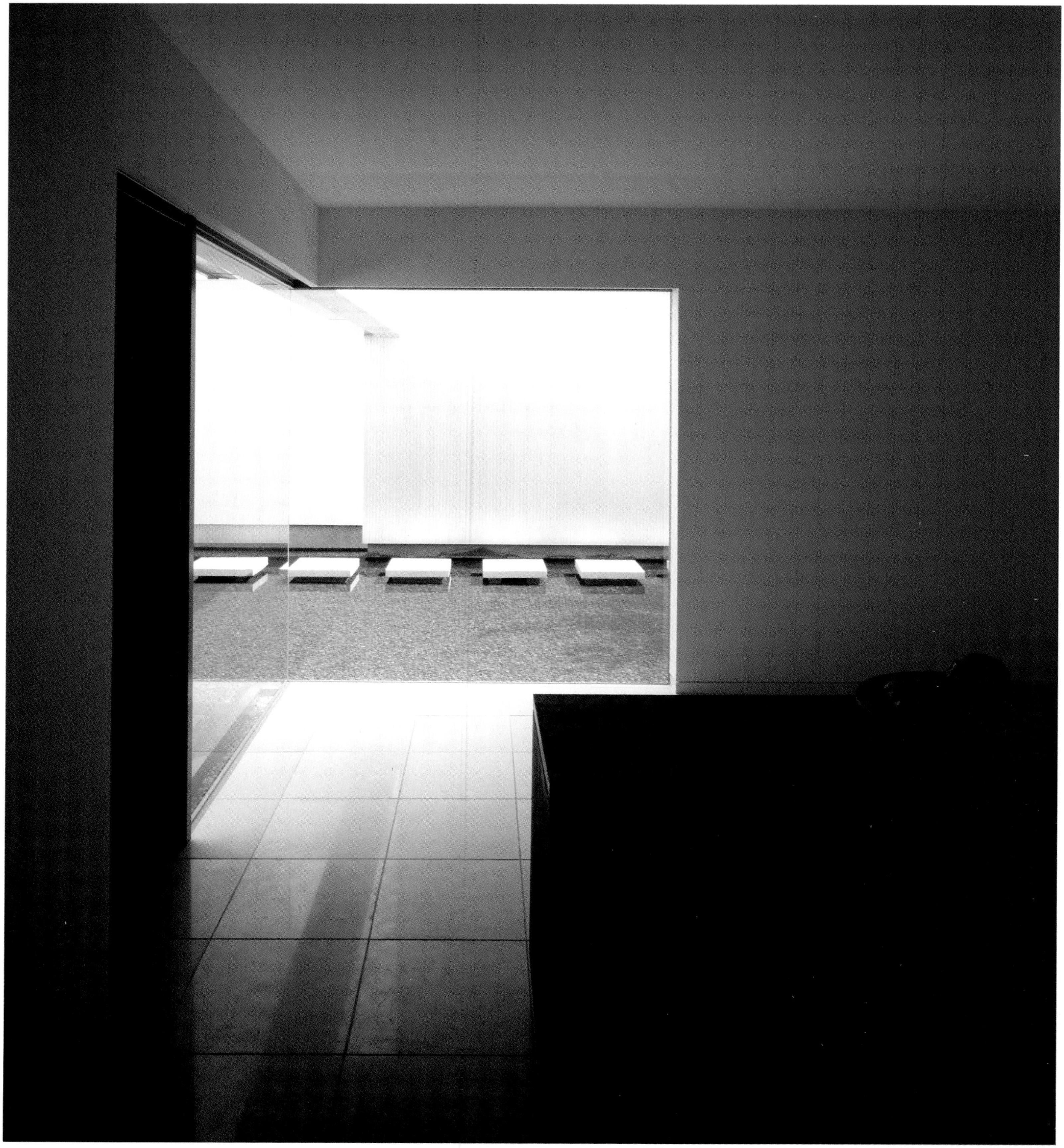

The new water garden becomes a forbidden space, only to be admired and not trespassed. The interior spaces are all geared toward this fundamental element of the home.

Roozen Beach House

The Roozen house is a new residence for a surfer and oil rig operator. The house, built elevated on a hill in a small cul-de-sac in the sand dunes of Margaret River, Western Australia, is oriented southwest, only 1,300 feet from the ocean. The building's architectural expression is an abstract interpretation of the magic of the site, which is played out in the building's plan through a series of framing devices that act as optical illusions as you journey through the building.

There are essentially three elements, which celebrate and orchestrate specific land-seascape views. One is the primary axis of the triangular site, directed toward the Indian Ocean. Another is the line of the Cape Leeuwin Ridge to the southeast, which forms

Architect: Dale Jones-Evans Pty Ltd
Collaborators: Matthew Chan, Jane Madeleine Pinfold
Photography: Ashley Jones-Evans, Stephen Blakney
Location: Margaret River, Cape Leeuwin Ridge, Western Australia
Date of construction: 2001
Area: 2,740 sq. ft.

another sea, and thirdly, a small cultural icon: a Greek church facing northwest. These elements are framed from within the different points in the structure as it anchors to the ground and projects out from this raw and beautiful landscape.

Designed as a simple cross form, the building affords a myriad of carefully considered internal and external spaces from which to reach out and retreat from the circumscribing land and seascape. In the living zone, a projectile platform made of steamed bamboo is oriented directly at Western Australia's premier big wave spot—the Bombie. These interior spaces are raw, minimal, and ascetic. Externally finished in raw cement render and a patina of ever greening copper, the building is like an old vessel cast into the landscape.

This structure, cast into the sloping terrain, juts out toward the sea like a vessel in search of its home. The building affords a myriad of carefully considered views of the ocean and mountains.

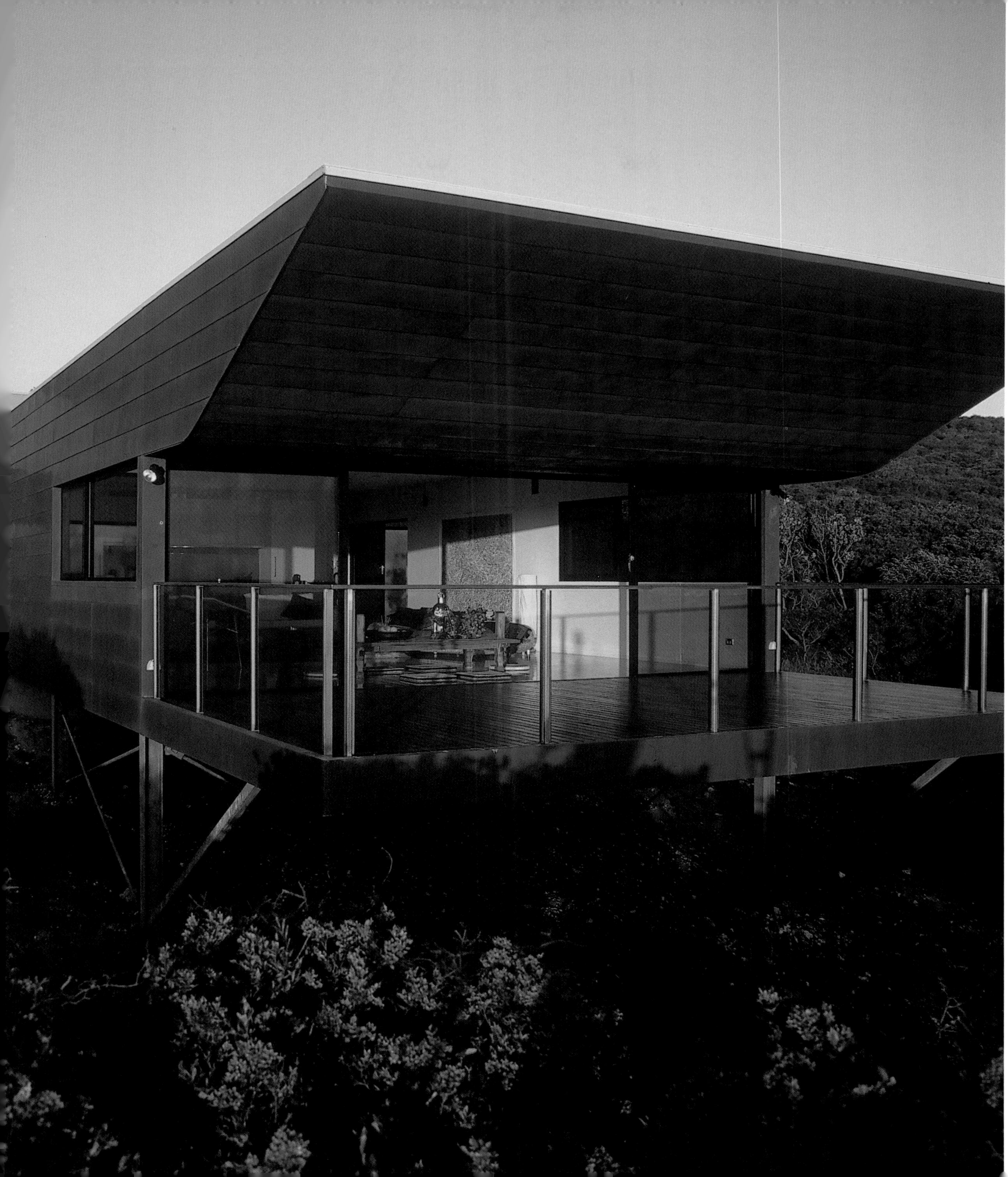

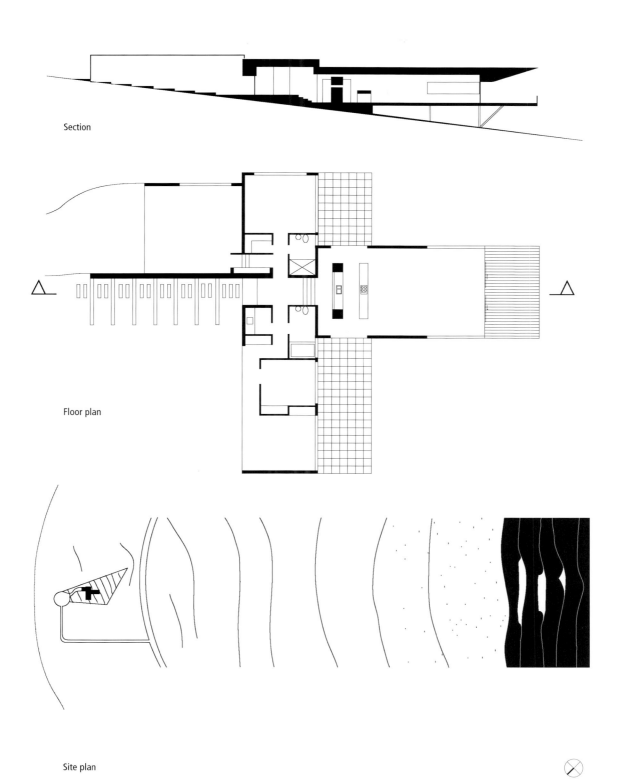

Section

Floor plan

Site plan

Mermaid Beach House

Situated on the Gold Coast of Queensland in Australia, this project involved the substantial renovation of an existing building composed of two independent structures. One of the requirements of the brief was to provide a physical connection between the two entities.

After the existing building was pared back, new and recycled timbers were used to link the front and rear sections of the house. The linking zone forms a central courtyard, comprised of an internal deck, fireplace, and plunge pool, allowing a respite from

Architect: Paul Uhlmann Architects Pty Ltd
Photography: David Sandison
Location: Mermaid Beach, Queensland, Australia
Date of construction: 2003
Area: 3,200 sq. ft.

inclement weather. The new courtyard allows a constant link with the ocean. Large recycled timber elements create a sculptural element on the ocean side that delineates the residence from the neighboring properties.

Paul Uhlmann Architects, an innovative design practice established in 1994, strives to achieve an architecture that is committed to producing exemplary design. Rather than having any particular style or fashion, the firm responds to the requirements of each client and site, deriving inspiration from the individuality of each project. Past projects express the diversity of the imagination and skill of Paul Uhlmann Architects and the desire to create individually expressive responses. These projects range from rural farm houses on Queensland's Sunshine Coast to urban residences in Canberra and commercial projects at Byron Bay. Paul Uhlmann Architects provide a personalized service from a team of dedicated design professionals who are committed to fulfilling the client's individual needs in a manner that becomes evident in the success of the building process and the beauty of the final product.

Large recycled timber elements create a sculptural element on the ocean side of the house that distinguishes the residence from its neighboring properties.

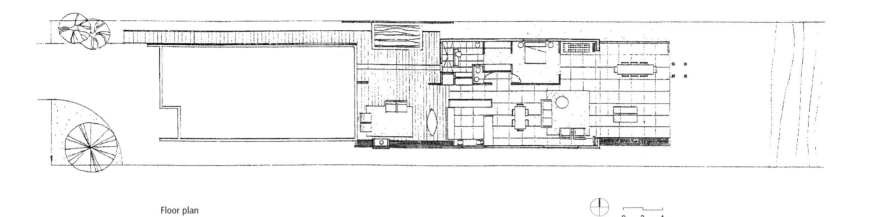

Floor plan

Cromer Residence

The client for this project was a young businessman who required three bedrooms, with the master bedroom incorporating a private TV room separate from the main living area. The composition of the building is comprised of a smaller ground floor, with cantilevered floors above that direct the building toward the view. The spine roof traverses the entire structure and terminates at a blade wall on the main deck, which was designed to provide a sense of privacy from the adjoining property.

Given the importance placed on the views to be obtained from the new design, one can see the water from every bedroom and living space. Because the living rooms are located on the first floor in an open plan, the kitchen was effectively

Architect: Jeremy Wolveridge Architect Pty Ltd
Collaborators: Stuart "Paul" Holmes, Peter Winkler
Photography: Shania Shegedyn
Location: Beaumaris, Melbourne, Victoria, Australia
Date of construction: 2003
Area: 4,000 sq. ft.

allocated to a core space separating the dining room, external deck, and sunken lounge. A kitchen bench sails over into the living area to serve as a high bar, reinforcing the connection between these two spaces. The private bedrooms are located on the upper levels.

The massing of forms is reminiscent of early 1950s coastal Australian architecture and derived from early modern architects such as Grounds and Boyd. Internally, the materials include dark stained timber joinery, hardwood floors and part plywood sheet ceilings with a predominantly drywall finish. Windows provide views of both the sea and the building itself from various angles. During the day, the natural light levels are in a state of constant change, providing a sense of movement and transformation within the spaces.

Massed cubes, cantilevered floors, and the materials employed are typical of coastal architecture in Australia and reminiscent of early modern architects of the area.

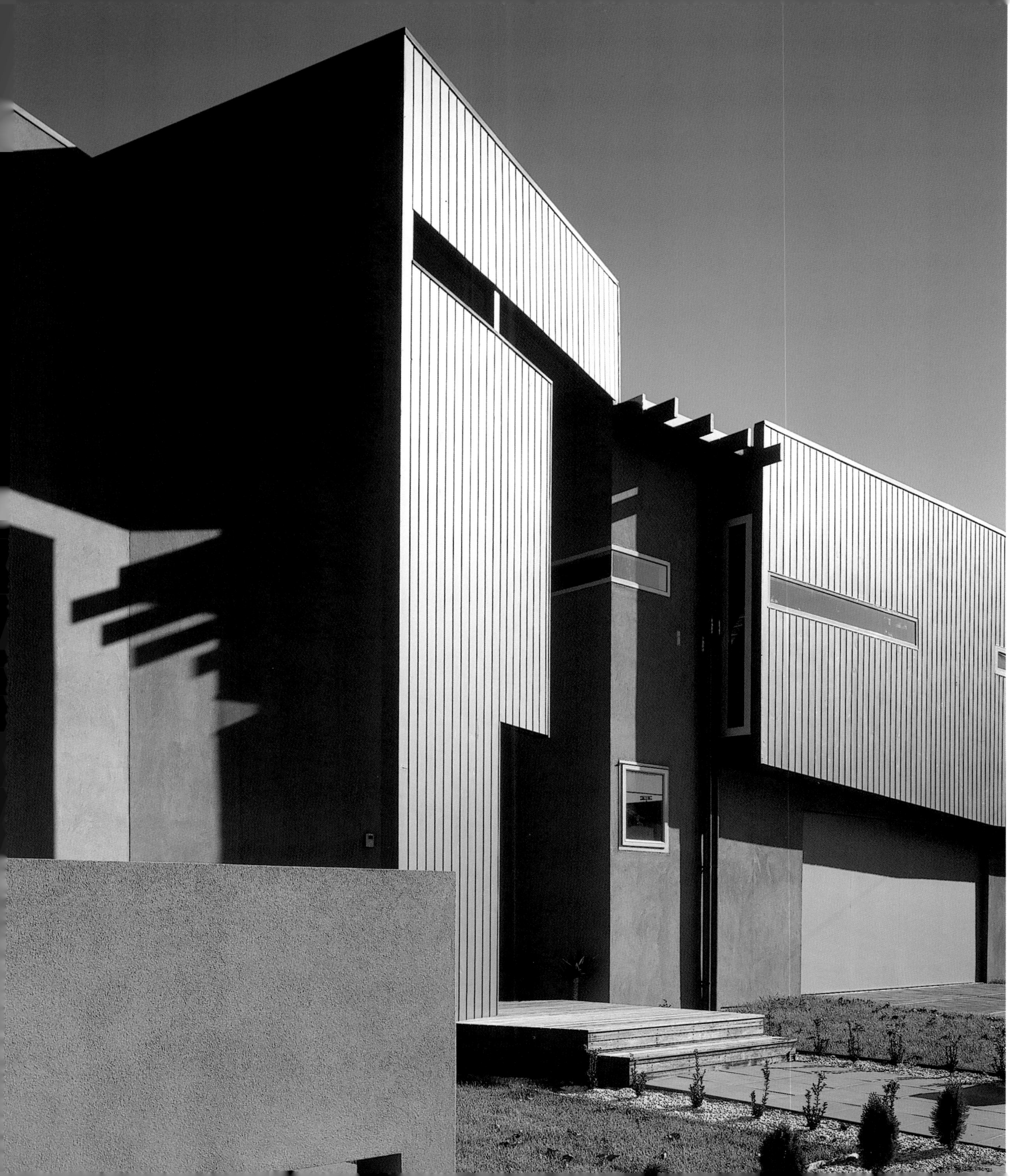

Windows provide views of both the sea and the building itself from various angles, while the orientation and configuration of the spaces provide varying light levels that generate a sense of movement within the spaces.

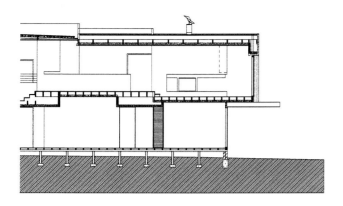

Sections

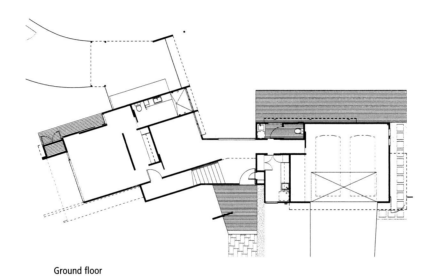

Ground floor

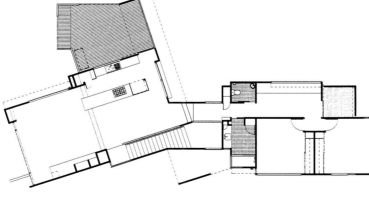

First floor

0　1　2

Materials inside the home include dark stained timber joinery, hardwood floors, and part plywood sheet ceilings with a predominantly drywall finish.

Pacific Palisades House

Originally designed by Richard Neutra for the screenwriters Benedict and Nancy Freedman in 1949, the small house sits on a large lot and is set back from the street, offering privacy and uninterrupted views of the ocean. Between 1959 and 1988, various architects completed several additions. The firm studio bau:ton took up the project in the mid-1990s, during which it completed exterior elements that were missing or in need of updating. Included was the completion of the hardscape, the addition of a garden shed, privacy walls, gates, entry stairs, and the landscaping. A reflecting pond by the entrance was also introduced, and the exterior siding was restored to its original stained redwood finish.

From 1999 to 2002, under different ownership, the addition of a second floor with two bedrooms and baths, an enlarged master bath area, and the remodeling of the kitchen were undertaken. The additions blend with the original structure, and the basic idea

Architect: studio bau:ton
Photography: John Ellis
Location: Pacific Palisades, California, USA
Date of construction: 2002
Area: 3,100 sq. ft.

of the open flow between interior and exterior is maintained and reinforced in all areas. The spatial quality and historical significance of the existing building were determining factors for the architectural approach and were well supported by both clients. While certain parts were restored to their original state, a conscious decision was made to design the new elements as integral parts of the original structure in an attempt to interpret the intent of the original design and extrapolate the inherent spatial and structural ideas.

The second floor achieves a dynamic of its own, with large window bands, roof overhangs, and detailing that is reminiscent of the original. Despite the significant change in the massing, the final composition results in a sense of continuity between the different generations of the building. The greater density contrasts with the open yard that slopes towards the ocean, made visible through the transparency of the living room.

This renowned house by Richard Neutra underwent a gradual renovation over the years, resulting in a sense of continuity between the different generations and an updated overall design.

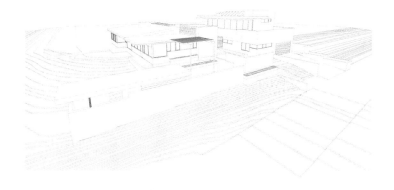

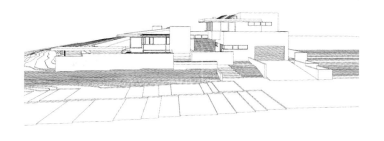

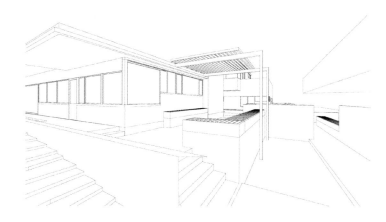

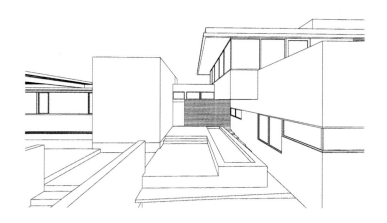

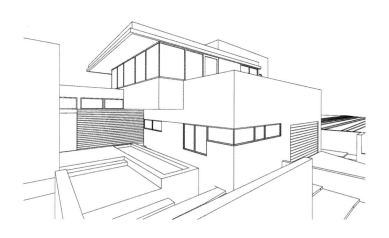

Perspectives

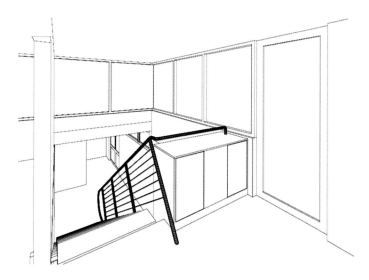

City Cube

City Cube is designed as a standard model plan of a three-story, urban residence with a concise structural system intended to reduce construction costs. The plan is a 30-foot square that is divided into small individual grids, enabling the segmentation of nine space volumes. The private areas, including the bedroom, bathroom, and guest room were allocated to the first floor. An office space was also created to allow the resident to work from home.

The top two floors are comprised of a steel-framed structure composed of four steel-framed columns and a wide flange that is used as sash bars on the periphery. On each of the two upper levels, eight of the segmented space volumes, excluding the center segment, can be combined in varying patterns according to family structure and use applications. In this case, the second floor is

Architect: Oishi Kazuhiku Architect Atelier
Photography: Kouji Okamoto
Location: Fukuoka, Japan
Date of construction: 2002
Area: 2,010 sq. ft.

created as a public space and two blocks on the third floor are allocated to the children's room, while the remaining space is left void with the intent to express the vertical expansion of urban dynamism in residential space.

The center of the plan is a tube of light penetrating the three levels into which a spiral stairway is built. The verticality of the stairway attempts to represent the transience of natural light produced by the movement of the sun and clouds through a translucent glass box, generating a sensible abstraction of natural phenomena. A deck is located along the south side of the second floor. A translucent glass screen secures privacy from the apartment building opposite, and softly shades off the surrounding cityscape that is made visible from the living room. Screens on the sides are left open as an intended gesture to show signs of the dweller's presence and to avoid disturbing the relationship with the surrounding long-established residential neighborhood. Through a cubic space within the urban environment, the creation of the building focuses on providing the dwellers comfortable living while experiencing a close relationship with the city and the surrounding nature.

This symmetrical structure was divided into a grid system that optimizes space and is distributed over three levels.
Private areas were situated on the first floor and third floor, with the public zones on the second level.

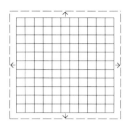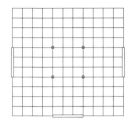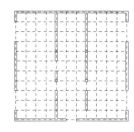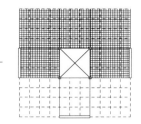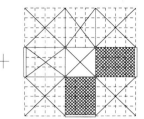

Details

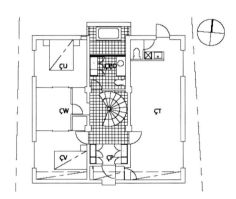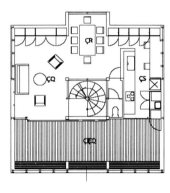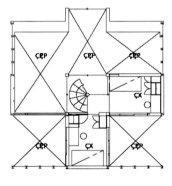

Ground floor

First floor

Second floor

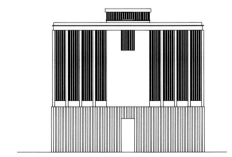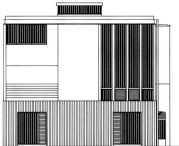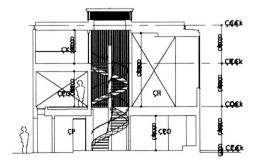

Elevations

Section

Belmont House

Unlike the mega McMansions of recent years that are built all over California and are prevalent in the San Francisco Bay area, this house is a particularly efficient, direct, and simple home. Owned by a young couple with a small child, the house is built into a hill in the city of Belmont near San Francisco. Unlike superficial historical reproductions, the project explores the fusion between two popular vernacular architectures of this region: the mobile-trailer home and the Mexican pueblo architecture. This vertical hybrid of two different cultures has inspired this new concept geared to younger generations living in the area.

A curved concrete retaining wall provides an edge for the driveway and directs the way uphill into the driveway. A series of concrete steps leads from the driveway to the mid-entry level. A long modern veranda with a blue stucco wall guides visitors to an

Architect: Hariri & Hariri - Architecture
Collaborators: Gisue Hariri & Mojgan Hariri, Principals; Marc Stierlin, Intern
Photography: Cesar Rubio
Location: Belmont, California, USA
Date of construction: 2002
Area: 3,000 sq. ft.

oversized rusted steel door. This dramatic entrance door pivots into the entrance hall where a staircase then takes one to the upper main floor.

Inspired by the Mexican pueblo architecture, the lower level of the house is composed of heavy walls with texture and color. A sculptural stair leads to the upper level, which contains the master suite on one end, a home office on the other, and a central area that combines the dining area, kitchen, and library. The upper level, more inspired by the industrial generation of mobile homes, is a rectangular volume wrapped in metal that floats over its solid base. Large openings on both the hill and the valley sides allow breezes to drift through the home and enable a panoramic view of the hillside. Ultimately, the paradoxical human desire to be part of the new and the old, the heavy and the light, the earth and the sky, the rooted and the mobile is expressed simultaneously.

The juxtaposition of styles, textures, and materials evokes a marriage between the old and the new, the heavy and the light, the anchored and the mobile—all in a coherent and dynamic structure.

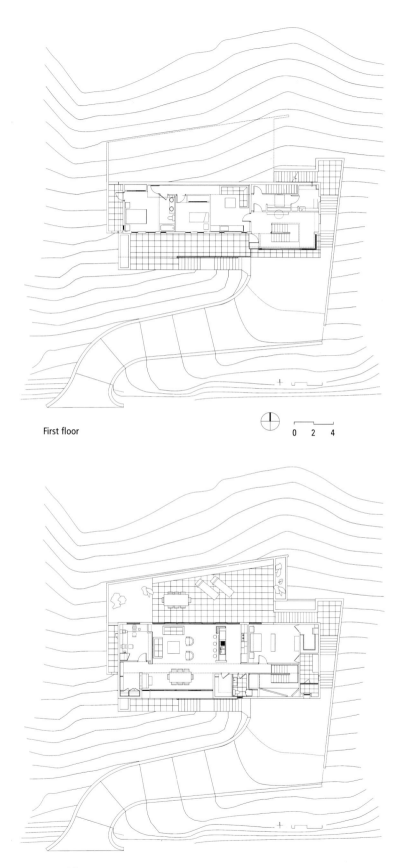

First floor

159

Second floor

Rose House

This house is located on a rural lot on the southern side of Saddleback Mountain, approximately 165 feet below the summit, enjoying views from the coastal escarpment in the west, Pigeon House Mountain in the south and the coastline to the east, including Werri Creek Lagoon and Seven Mile Beach. The view to the north is of the heavily forested hillside leading up to Saddleback Mountain Lookout. In order to maximize the views and build on the more gentle slope, the house was erected adjacent to the road at the upper edge of the site and centered to take advantage of an almost symmetrical fall to both the east and the west.

The rectangular plan is divided into three areas by way of two service cores. The east wing is designated to the parents and the west wing to the children, while the kitchen, living, and dining areas are situated in between. By centering the living areas and pulling the service cores toward the back, significant views can be obtained from different points within the house. When the

Architect: Engelen Moore Pty Ltd
Collaborators: Dua Cox, Claire Meller, Sterrin O'Shea
Photography: Ross Honeysett
Location: Saddleback Mountain, New South Wales, Australia
Date of construction: 1998
Area: 4,050 sq. ft.

house is entered, the dramatic view down the mountain to the south is instantly apparent. Wide decks run the length of the house on both the north and the south, providing both shade and weather protection for the large sliding glass walls. When the doors are open, the entire living area becomes an open veranda space, with exceptional cross ventilation.

In order to minimize the impact of the building on the site, a lightweight steel structure was adopted, consisting of two Vierendeel trusses running the length of the house atop two reinforced concrete block storerooms anchored to the ground. The trusses allow the house to cantilever beyond the storerooms at the east and west ends, while the two service cores pass through the floor down to ground level, bracing the structure. These cores also conceal all plumbing installations and provide storage areas beneath the house. The roof and walls are clad in steel sheeting, while the window and door system consists of identical sliding aluminum framed glass doors.

To minimize the impact of the new structure on the virgin site, a lightweight steel material was chosen to fabricate two Vierendeel trusses running the length of the house atop two reinforced concrete blocks anchored to the ground.

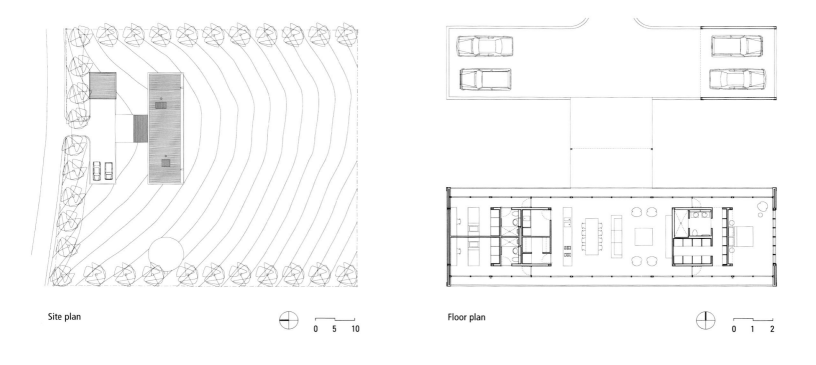

Site plan

0 5 10

Floor plan

0 1 2

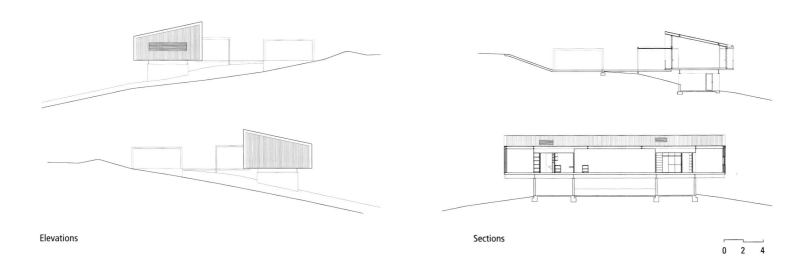

Elevations

Sections

0 2 4

Directory

Belzberg Architects
1655 Stanford Street
Santa Monica, CA 90404
T: +1 310 453 9611
F: +1 310 453 9166
www.belzbergarchitects.com

Dale Jones-Evans Pty Ltd
Loft 1, 50-54 Ann Street
Surry Hills, NSW 2010
Australia
T: +61 2 9211 0626
F: +61 2 9211 5998
www.dje.com.au

Engelen Moore Pty Ltd
44 McLachlan Avenue
Rushcutters Bay
Sydney, NSW 2011
Australia
T: +61 2 9380 4099
F: +61 2 9380 4302
www.engelenmoore.com.au

Enrique Muller
Río Chico 32
Colonia Puente Colorado
Mexico D.F., 01730
T: +52 56 35 34 42
F: +52 56 35 34 12
eclectica@prodigy.net.mx

Eric Rosen Architects Inc
11525 Washington Boulevard
Los Angeles, CA 90066
T: +1 310 313 3052
F: +1 310 313 3062
www.ericrosen.com

Farnan Findlay Architects
6 Boronia Street
Redfern, NSW 2016
Australia
T: +61 2 9310 2516
F: +61 2 9310 2517
farnan_findlay@bigpond.com

Hariri & Hariri - Architecture
18 East 12th Street
New York, NY 10003
T: +1 212 727 0338
F: +1 212 727 0479
www.haririandhariri.com

Hayball Leonard Stent Architects Pty Ltd
135 Sturt Street, Suite 4
Southbank, Victoria 3006
Australia
T: +61 3 9699 3644
F: +61 3 9699 3708
www.hayball.com.au

Jeremy Wolveridge Architect Pty Ltd
83-87 Dover Street, Unit 9
Richmond, Victoria 3121
Australia
T: +61 3 9425 9977
F: +61 3 9427 8266
www.jwarchitect.com.au

Lahz Nimmo Architects
Level 5, 116-122 Kippax Street
Surry Hills, NSW 2010
Australia
T: +61 2 9211 1220
F: +61 2 9211 1554
www.lahznimmo.com

Leddy Maytum Stacy Architects
677 Harrison Street
San Francisco, CA 94107
T: +1 415 495 1700
F: +1 415 496 1717
www.lmsarch.com

Moore Ruble Yudell Architects & Planners
933 Pico Boulevard
Santa Monica, CA 90405
T: +1 310 450 1400
F: +1 310 450 1403
www.mryarchitects.com

Oishi Kazuhiko Architect Atelier
7-2-7 Nishijin Sawaraku Fukuokasi
Fukuoka Japan
T: +81 92 823 0882
F: +81 92 823 0925
oishi.architect@jcom.home.ne.jp

Paul Uhlmann Architects Pty Ltd
24/66 Goodwin Terrace
Burleigh Heads, Queensland 4220
Australia
T: +61 7 5576 7321

Ronald Frink Architects Inc
2439 West Silver Lake Drive
Los Angeles, CA 90039
T: +1 323 662 0040
F: +1 323 662 2955

Shubin + Donaldson Architects Inc
3834 Willat Avenue
Culver City, CA 90232
T: +1 310 204 0688
F: +1 310 204 0219

studio bau:ton
3780 Wilshire Boulevard, Suite 202
Los Angeles, CA 90010
T: +1 213 251-9791
F: +1 213 251-9795
www.bauton.com

Waro Kishi + K. ASSOCIATES/Architects
4F Yukata Bldg. 366 Karigane-cho
Nakagyo-ku
Kyoto, 604-8115
Japan
T: +81 75 213 0258
F: +81 75 213 0259
www.k-associates.com